SandCastle

Rhyme Time

The Bale of Mail

Jan Westberg

Consulting Editor, Diane Craig, M.A./Reading Specialist

ABDO
Publishing Company

Published by ABDO Publishing Company, 4940 Viking Drive, Edina, Minnesota 55435.

Printed in the United States.

Credits
Edited by: Pam Price
Curriculum Coordinator: Nancy Tuminelly
Cover and Interior Design and Production: Mighty Media
Photo and Illustration Credits: BananaStock Ltd., Brand X Pictures, Hemera, Image 100, Tracy Kompelien, PhotoDisc, Rubberball Productions, Stockbyte

Library of Congress Cataloging-in-Publication Data

Westberg, Jan.
    The bale of mail / Jan Westberg.
      p. cm. -- (Rhyme time)
    Includes index.
    ISBN 1-59197-775-4 (hardcover)
    ISBN 1-59197-881-5 (paperback)
    1. English language--Rhyme--Juvenile literature. I. Title. II. Rhyme time (ABDO Publishing Company)

PE1517.W473 2004
428.1'3--dc22
                                                            2004047246

SandCastle™ books are created by a professional team of educators, reading specialists, and content developers around five essential components that include phonemic awareness, phonics, vocabulary, text comprehension, and fluency. All books are written, reviewed, and leveled for guided reading, early intervention reading, and Accelerated Reader® programs and designed for use in shared, guided, and independent reading and writing activities to support a balanced approach to literacy instruction.

Let Us Know

After reading the book, SandCastle would like you to tell us your stories about reading. What is your favorite page? Was there something hard that you needed help with? Share the ups and downs of learning to read. We want to hear from you! To get posted on the ABDO Publishing Company Web site, send us e-mail at:

sandcastle@abdopub.com

SandCastle Level: Transitional

Words that rhyme do
not have to be spelled the
same. These words rhyme
with each other:

bale   sale

fail   scale

mail   tail

pale   veil

rail   wail

Joel does his homework every night without fail.

Annie is standing next to a bale of hay.

Dave likes to be the one who gets his family's mail.

Mike's family is moving, so their house is for sale.

Barb sits on the steps and Jan holds onto the rail.

Amelia's skin tone is **pale**.

When a dog is happy, it wags its tail.

Scott likes to **scale** the rope ladder.

Ronnie lets out a big **wail**.

Lisa is playing dress up.

She's wearing a **veil**.

The Bale of Mail

Gail's job is to deliver mail.
To deliver the mail, you cannot be frail.

Gail sorts a ton of mail
and weighs it on a scale.

She does her job to the last detail.

Some days she would wail,
"Just where should I leave your mail?"

Where, oh where?

The farmer wants his mail
to be left on top of a big hay bale.

Mrs. Dale wants her mail
to be hidden behind a pale veil.

The police want their mail
to be put on the bench
outside the jail.

Whatever the tale, Gail will never fail to deliver the bale of mail.

She will not be stopped by a gale, or even by snow, sleet, or hail!

Rhyming Riddle

What do you call a machine that weighs frozen rain?

Hail scale

Glossary

bale. a large bundle of goods tied tightly together

frail. physically weak

scale. to climb; a machine for weighing things

veil. a piece of cloth that covers a woman's head, shoulders, and face

wail. a long cry of sadness or pain

About SandCastle™

A professional team of educators, reading specialists, and content developers created the SandCastle™ series to support young readers as they develop reading skills and strategies and increase their general knowledge. The SandCastle™ series has four levels that correspond to early literacy development in young children. The levels are provided to help teachers and parents select the appropriate books for young readers.

Emerging Readers
(no flags)

Beginning Readers
(1 flag)

Transitional Readers
(2 flags)

Fluent Readers
(3 flags)

These levels are meant only as a guide. All levels are subject to change.

ABDO
Publishing Company

To see a complete list of SandCastle™ books and other nonfiction titles from ABDO Publishing Company, visit www.abdopub.com or contact us at:
4940 Viking Drive, Edina, Minnesota 55435 • 1-800-800-1312 • fax: 1-952-831-1632